PLAYALONG

VIOLIN

Showstoppers

Violin part

Arranged by David Gedge

Bosworth
8/9 Frith Street
London W1D 3JB

Music processed by Camden Music.
Original Cover Design by Ian Butterworth.
Printed in Great Britain.

ALL I ASK OF YOU
(from 'The Phantom Of The Opera')

Words by Charles Hart
Music by Andrew Lloyd Webber

GETTING TO KNOW YOU

Words by Oscar Hammerstein II
Music by Richard Rodgers

HOPELESSLY DEVOTED TO YOU

Words & Music by John Farrar

In the style of a 1950s rock 'n' roll ballad

to Coda $\oplus$

D.S. al Coda

$\oplus$ Coda

I'D DO ANYTHING

Words & Music by Lionel Bart

MAMMA MIA

Words & Music by Benny Andersson, Bjorn Ulvaeus & Stig Anderson

THE LAST NIGHT OF THE WORLD
(from 'Miss Saigon')

Words by Alain Boublil & Richard Maltby Jr.
Music by Claude-Michel Schönberg

MIRACLE OF MIRACLES

Words by Sheldon Harnick
Music by Jerry Bock

THE MUSIC OF THE NIGHT
(from 'The Phantom Of The Opera')

Words by Charles Hart
Music by Andrew Lloyd Webber

ON MY OWN
(from 'Les Misérables')

Words by Alain Boublil & Jean-Marc Natel
Music by Claude-Michel Schönberg

SOME ENCHANTED EVENING

Words by Oscar Hammerstein II
Music by Richard Rodgers

PLAYALONG

VIOLIN

Showstoppers

Arranged by David Gedge

Bosworth
8/9 Frith Street
London W1D 3JB

This book © Copyright 2004 Bosworth.
Order No. BOE005189 ISBN 1-84449-279-6

Music processed by Camden Music.
Original Cover Design by Ian Butterworth.
Printed in Great Britain.

CD recorded, mixed and mastered by Jonas Persson.
Solo violin: Dermot Crehan.

Backing Tracks:
'All I Ask Of You' and 'I'd Do Anything' by John Maul;
'Getting To Know You', 'The Music Of The Night' and 'On My Own' by Music By Design;
'Hopelessly Devoted To You' and 'The Last Night Of The World' by Danny G;
'Mamma Mia' and 'Some Enchanted Evening' by Paul Honey;
'Miracle Of Miracles' by Rick Cardinali.

ALL I ASK OF YOU
(from 'The Phantom Of The Opera')

Words by Charles Hart
Music by Andrew Lloyd Webber

GETTING TO KNOW YOU

Words by Oscar Hammerstein II
Music by Richard Rodgers

senza pedal

senza pedal

HOPELESSLY DEVOTED TO YOU

Words & Music by John Farrar

In the style of a 1950s rock 'n' roll ballad

Use pedal where appropriate to sustain chords.

to Coda ⊕

D.S. al Coda

Coda

I'D DO ANYTHING

Words & Music by Lionel Bart

THE LAST NIGHT OF THE WORLD
(from 'Miss Saigon')

Words by Alain Boublil & Richard Maltby Jr.
Music by Claude-Michel Schönberg

PLAYALONG

VIOLIN
Showstoppers

Violin part
Arranged by David Gedge

Bosworth
8/9 Frith Street
London W1D 3JB

Music processed by Camden Music.
Original Cover Design by Ian Butterworth.
Printed in Great Britain.

ALL I ASK OF YOU
(from 'The Phantom Of The Opera')

Words by Charles Hart
Music by Andrew Lloyd Webber

GETTING TO KNOW YOU

Words by Oscar Hammerstein II
Music by Richard Rodgers

HOPELESSLY DEVOTED TO YOU

Words & Music by John Farrar

In the style of a 1950s rock 'n' roll ballad

I'D DO ANYTHING

Words & Music by Lionel Bart

MAMMA MIA

Words & Music by Benny Andersson, Bjorn Ulvaeus & Stig Anderson

THE LAST NIGHT OF THE WORLD
(from 'Miss Saigon')

Words by Alain Boublil & Richard Maltby Jr.
Music by Claude-Michel Schönberg

MIRACLE OF MIRACLES

Words by Sheldon Harnick
Music by Jerry Bock

12

THE MUSIC OF THE NIGHT
(from 'The Phantom Of The Opera')

Words by Charles Hart
Music by Andrew Lloyd Webber

ON MY OWN
(from 'Les Misérables')

Words by Alain Boublil & Jean-Marc Natel
Music by Claude-Michel Schönberg

SOME ENCHANTED EVENING

Words by Oscar Hammerstein II
Music by Richard Rodgers

MAMMA MIA

Words & Music by Benny Andersson, Bjorn Ulvaeus & Stig Anderson

D.S.

pizz.

Repeat to fade

THE MUSIC OF THE NIGHT
(from 'The Phantom Of The Opera')

Words by Charles Hart
Music by Andrew Lloyd Webber

Moderato, gently and with rubato

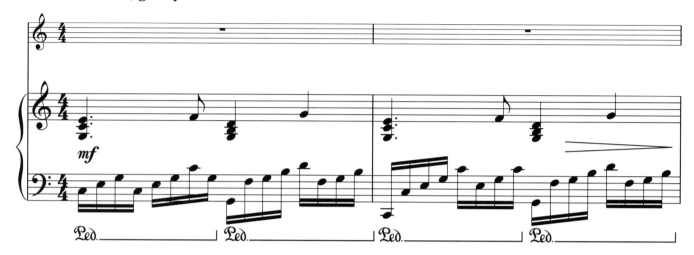

ON MY OWN
(from 'Les Misérables')

Words by Alain Boublil & Jean-Marc Natel
Music by Claude-Michel Schönberg

Sadly, expressively and with rubato

rall. e dim.   **a tempo**

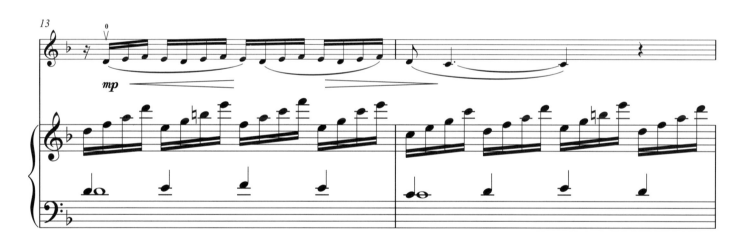

(3rd position preferable)   (back to 1st position)

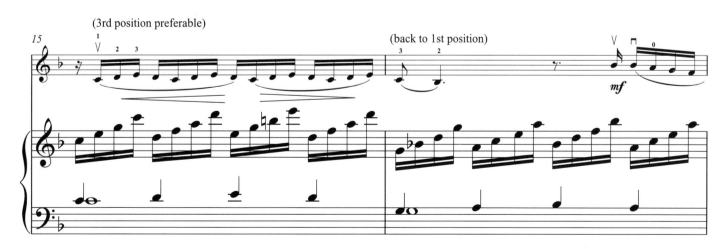

rall.   a tempo; relaxed speed but no rubato

SOME ENCHANTED EVENING

Words by Oscar Hammerstein II
Music by Richard Rodgers

MIRACLE OF MIRACLES

Words by Sheldon Harnick
Music by Jerry Bock